EXPLAINING
Eternally secure?
What the Bible says about being saved

DAVID PAWSON

ANCHOR RECORDINGS

First published in Great Britain in 2016 by
Anchor Recordings Ltd
Synegis House, 21 Crockhamwell Road,
Woodley, Reading RG5 3LE

**For more of David Pawson's teaching,
including DVDs and CDs, go to
www.davidpawson.com**

**FOR FREE DOWNLOADS
www.davidpawson.org**

**For further information,
email: info@davidpawsonministry.com**

ISBN 978-1-911173-19-9

Printed by Lightning Source

This booklet is based on a talk. Originating as it does from the spoken word, its style will be found by many readers to be somewhat different from my usual written style. It is hoped that this will not detract from the substance of the biblical teaching found here.

As always, I ask the reader to compare everything I say or write with what is written in the Bible and, if at any point a conflict is found, always to rely upon the clear teaching of scripture.

David Pawson

EXPLAINING
Eternally secure?
What the Bible says about being saved

My book entitled *The Road to Hell* was advertised in a national magazine in England in these words: "Read David Pawson's autobiography, *The Road to Hell*". Actually, that book was a miracle. I was going to Italy to speak at a conference, and I had a big case with my clothes in and a little black briefcase. Inside the briefcase was the entire manuscript of the book. I write all my books with a fountain pen and there was only one manuscript of it. When I got to the airport in Bologna it was midnight. It was dark and the rain was pouring down, and we went to the car park. The pastor meeting me said, "Get into the car, and I'll put your luggage in the back of the car." We got to his house an hour later, and he opened the trunk and pulled out my case and then closed the trunk. I said, "Just a minute, there's my briefcase."

"No," he replied, "There was only the case." He hadn't seen the black briefcase on the luggage trolley because it was so dark and wet.

"But," I said, "all my notes for the conference are in that briefcase, and a manuscript of a whole book called *The Road to Hell*." We dashed back to the airport at one o'clock in the morning. There was no sign of the briefcase, no sign of the luggage trolley. We went to the lost property office. They had not had it handed in. We went to the police and said,

"We've lost a briefcase," and the police smiled and said, "You lost a briefcase in Italy?" – as much as to say that's the last you'll see of it.

I was actually sleeping in a garage that night, and I knelt down by a camp bed and said, "Lord, you've given me a wonderful opportunity to find out if you want that book published. If you want it published, you'll have to find it and bring it back because I'm not going to write it again. If you don't want it published, I don't want it back." The next day I drove a hundred miles to the Adriatic Coast to the conference hotel. Early in the morning I went for a lovely walk on the beach. A friendly dog joined me and we had a good time together. I came back to the hotel and a man walked up to me and put my briefcase in my hand. To this day we do not know who he was or where he had been. This was a hundred miles away, the next morning! I opened it, and all the manuscript was there, but the pages had been put into the wrong order. It took me about half an hour to put the pages in the right order, but none was missing. That is how that book came to be published, so I am sure God wanted me to publish it. It is not a popular subject.

It is another book I am thinking about now. *Once Saved, Always Saved* was written by a good friend of mine, Dr. R. T. Kendall, of whom I am sure you will have heard. I published a book of the same title with the addition of a question mark – we differ on this point.

In my short book on Grace, I explained grace and saving grace. There I pointed out that there are two other views of grace: one called *sovereign* grace, one called *free* grace. One matter on which they both agree is "once saved, always saved", but for entirely different reasons. "Sovereign grace" says that grace is irresistible. It will force you to be saved, and it will force you to be kept. It will force you to the point where you are completely saved, and you can do nothing about that. God has decided. He has chosen you, and therefore, you will be "once saved, always saved". "Free grace" also agrees to that. "Free grace" comes more from the dispensational school, while "sovereign grace" comes from the Calvinist or Reformed school. "Free grace" also says when you come to Christ not only are all your past sins forgiven, but all your future sins are forgiven, too. Therefore, nothing you can do can stop the process of salvation. Whatever you do, it is all already signed, sealed, and delivered. You are saved.

I guess that my quarrel with that phrase is not only that it is not in the Bible, but I don't agree with the first part of it. That is my problem: *I am not once saved yet*, therefore I am not *always* saved yet. One day I am going to shout as loudly as I can, "I'm once saved, so I'm always saved" – but I can't say it yet. When my salvation is complete, when my wife's husband is perfect, then I'm going to shout, "Once saved, always saved!" The most important thing (I am going to repeat myself quite a bit here) is what you think "saved" means. In my understanding it means to be free from all sins, and to be exactly what God meant me to be when he made me – restored to the perfect image of God. Since Christ is the perfect image of God, it means I shall actually be like Jesus. That is the objective of salvation. God wants to restore us.

All that comes from the very beginning of creation, because one of the questions that we need to ask is: "Why did God make us?" That is a very important question. The answer is: he already had one Son, and he enjoyed that so much that he wanted a bigger family. I can't explain more simply why God created you and me. God wanted a bigger family like his Son. Until we are like his Son, God can't fully enjoy that family. His own Son was so trusting and obedient; then, when we are perfect in love too, he can fully enjoy family life with us. That is why he made the world. That is why he made us. You can understand that. Parents who love their child usually want another like the first. That was God's intention in creation. When you go right to the end of history you find the other end of that purpose, because you find that God's intention is to make a brand-new universe that will never know sin, that will never be polluted, that will never be spoiled by war. He has written off this present universe, and he is going to make another one. Therefore, if he is going to put people in it, he must make them perfect before he does. Otherwise it will be the same as this one.

I heard a story of a professor who invented a television set that you could tune into the future to see what was going to happen. He gathered people around for the first time to demonstrate his new television and they asked him to switch ahead thirty years. He fiddled with the knob to thirty and the picture came, and they all gasped. The whole earth was devastated. There was nothing but ash everywhere as far as the eye could see. There had clearly been a nuclear holocaust, and everything had gone. The people there stared at this screen, and then to their surprise the ash began to stir a little, and out from the ash came a little boy monkey. He looked around and he said, "They've done it, haven't they? I'm the only bit of life left." He sat there looking very miserable and depressed when suddenly, just a few metres away, the ash stirred again, and out came a little female monkey. The male monkey thought, "Life's not so bad." He went up to her and took her by the paw and said, "Look what people have done to our world." He said, "We'll have nothing to eat." She said, "Well, I've got something. I've managed to save something." She opened her paw and here was a little apple. The male monkey looked at it and said, "Don't let's begin that all over again."

When we look ahead we see a new heaven and a new earth and new people to inhabit it – people who will never spoil it; a place where there is no sin and no temptation, and everything can be enjoyed to the full. That is God's idea. He meant the garden of Eden to be like that, but it got spoiled so quickly. He is going to do it again, but this time he is prepared to take people who have spoiled this world and make them into creatures restored to his image and now perfect and able to look after his world properly. That is a great idea, and that is the future. So whether we look at the beginning of creation or the future of a new creation, we see God's plan and purpose all the way through of having a larger family who will please him and with whom he can have real fellowship. That is God's purpose.

That is why I want to underline again that salvation is *a process which takes time*. It is a process of taking old, sinful people like us and making us into new people. That is because God loved us. He could have said, "I'm going to wipe out this world and wipe out all the people in it and start again." He could do that. He once nearly did it in the days of Noah's flood. He wiped out that generation, but he saved one family. Alas, one of the first things Noah did when he got out of the ark was to get drunk and expose himself to his own son. The whole sad story started again. It is almost as if God said: right, that doesn't work, I'll have a better plan than that. The plan was to save sinners and make them into saints and then make the new world.

Do you realise that creation is happening again, but in reverse order? In the first creation, he made the heavens and the earth, and then he put the people in it later. This time around, he is making new people first. When he has got enough new people ready, he will make a new heaven and a new earth last. We are now in the second week of creation – God has gone back to work and he is creating again. Incidentally, that is one reason why we worship on a Sunday and not on a Saturday. The Jews worship on a Saturday to celebrate the finish of his old creation. We worship on a Sunday to celebrate the beginning of a new creation.

"Once saved, always saved? What does it mean to be "once saved"? I have already told you it means to be perfect. It means to be the person God wanted you to be. That is going to take him time and take us time. The three stages of salvation are: when we are set free from the *penalty* of sin, which we call "justification"; when we are set free from the *power* of sin, which we call "sanctification"; and when we are set free from the *possibility* of sin – that is called "glorification". Those are the three steps which God intends, and *all of them comprise salvation.* You cannot say "I'm once saved" until you reach all three. It will probably coincide with the Lord's return to earth. There is a verse in Hebrews which says that he will appear a second time not to deal with sin but to bring salvation to those who are waiting for him – and I am waiting for him. That is future, and I am waiting for my salvation. I am looking forward to being saved, and that is when I am going to shout, "Once saved, always saved" – when the work is complete. If you say it before then you think the work has passed. When you use the verb "save" only in the past tense, looking back, and say "I was saved then", you are talking as if it is finished, as if it is all complete. I teach people never to say "I was saved there and then," but to say: "I *began* to be saved there and then." What a difference it makes to your thinking when you say that.

I began to be saved in 1947, and yet it is obvious to anyone who knows me that it is not complete yet, particularly to my wife. She knows I am not there yet, but she knows that I am not what I was. I love the man who prayed, "Lord, I'm not what I ought to be. I'm not what I'm going to be, but praise the Lord! I am not what I was!" That is where we all are. I am not where I ought to be yet. I am not what I am going to be, but praise the Lord I am not what I was! That is the process of salvation that God is doing. He is doing a good work in me, and he will complete the work that he has begun provided I co-operate with him.

You see, the question is: can I interrupt the process of salvation? Can I delay it? Can I stop it altogether, or, as people generally ask, "Can I lose my salvation?" Well, if you haven't got it all yet, you can't lose it all, but you have *started* being saved. Can you lose that, or is it automatic, inevitable, that it will be completed?

Notice that whenever the scripture talks about the process being completed there is an expression not of certainty, but of confidence. Paul, writing to the Philippians, says, "I am confident that the Lord who began a good work in you will complete it against that day." The letter to the Hebrews does the same thing. After giving a solemn warning that those who go back cannot return because they cannot repent, he then adds: "But I am confident that this won't happen to you." Now that is *not* saying, "I'm certain it won't." It is saying, "I have high hopes that in your case the job will be completed." We need to notice that word: *confident*. It is not the word "certain". Its meaning is: I have high hopes that in your case it will be completed.

We should do a bit more Bible study and look at some of the passages which teach that the process of salvation can be interrupted and delayed and even stopped altogether so that it never is completed. Do you find that in your Bible? There are eighty separate passages in the New Testament warning you not to allow the process to stop. Every writer of the New Testament has a warning to Christians not to lose what they have found in Christ. Eighty is enough for me!

Those warning passages are rarely taught by preachers. We love the texts that give us assurance of the future. We love such texts as "I am persuaded that neither death nor life, neither angels nor principalities, neither powers, neither things present nor things to come, neither height nor depth, nor anything else can separate us from the love of God in Christ Jesus." That is at the end of Romans 8, and you will hear that quoted again and again. What preachers don't point out is that there is one thing missing from that list of things that cannot separate us from God's love, and that is *yourself*. Did you ever notice that? When Jesus said, "No one can snatch you from my hand," he did not say that you can't jump out of his hand. All those lists of things that cannot prevent us from staying in God's love don't include yourself – not one of them. It is a comfort to know that nothing else and no one else can stop the process of salvation, but *you* can. That is the serious thing that I am teaching here.

Scripture invariably balances up the picture, and when there is a verse like that it isn't far away that you will find another verse that says something very different. One of the passages out of those eighty in the New Testament is in Romans 11 – "And if you do not continue in God's kindness, you too will be cut off" – like many of the Jews were cut off. That is only on the next page after that wonderful statement in Romans 8. Now this is the problem with our Bible. God didn't put chapter and verse numbers in it. Therefore you can't quote references if you have a Bible without verses and chapter numbers. Did you know there was one published? You can now get the New International Version without chapter numbers and without verse numbers. A friend of mine, a professor of law in a university in Malibu in California, produced that Bible with no chapter and verse numbers in it. I hope you will get a copy because you will have to know your Bible a bit better. To find anything in the Bible you have to know the context, and you have to read the context. You can't pick out a text as a kind of proof for a doctrine. You have to take the text in its context.

I have noticed in the Bible wherever there is a verse that tells us that he is able to keep us, there is another verse that tells us we must keep ourselves. What a balance! Take the little letter of Jude. At the end of the letter of Jude it says, "God is able to keep you and present you faultless before his throne of majesty." He is able to, but just three verses up from that wonderful promise there is another verse that says "Keep yourselves in the love of God." There is the balance, and if you only quote one of those two texts you are unbalanced. Take Paul's letters to Timothy. In one verse he says: "He is able to keep what I've committed to him." If you only read that verse, you will not read the companion verse just about on the same page that says, "I have kept the faith." Keeping going is a co-operation between you and God. He is able to keep and you are to keep.

This balance is everywhere in scripture, but if you only quote text you come out with a one-sided balance – imbalance. Wherever we read about God's keeping power you will find an exhortation to keep yourself. As we keep ourselves in the love of God, he keeps what we have committed to him. That is the balance. That is the whole truth and not a dangerous half-truth. So there is a responsibility on us to go on co-operating with God, to go on believing in him, to go on responding to his kindness, to go on to the end and endure. It is those who endure to the end who are saved. In other words, to put it quite bluntly: *It is not those who start the Christian life who get saved, but those who finish in faith*. What a lesson that is! Many, many people start but they don't finish. The New Testament is full of warnings to those who start and don't finish. Faith is a continual relationship of trust and obedience. As long as we keep in the faith, he will keep us.

Let us look at one or two of the passages out of those eighty which say this kind of thing. I have already mentioned

Romans, but let me start in the Gospels. What about John 15? "I am the true vine," said Jesus. "And my Father is the gardener. He cuts off every branch in me that bears no fruit, while every branch that does bear fruit he trims clean so that it will be even more fruitful. You are already clean because of the word I have spoken to you." Now he says, "Remain in me, and I will remain in you." There is the balance again. You stay in me, and I'll stay in you, but the underlying warning is: if you don't stay in me, I won't stay in you. There it is, so what will happen if we don't remain? "No branch can bear fruit by itself; it must remain in the vine. Neither can you bear fruit unless you remain in me. I am the vine; you are the branches. If a man remains in me and I in him, he will bear much fruit; apart from me you can do nothing." Now the warning: "If anyone does not remain in me, he is like a branch that is thrown away and withers; such branches are picked up, thrown into the fire and burned. If you remain in me and my words remain in you, ask whatever you wish, and it will be given you. This is to my Father's glory, that you bear much fruit, showing yourselves to be my disciples." There it is very clear. You remain, you stay, you live in me and I will remain in you, and we'll produce fruit together.

Can I say this very clearly: eternal life is not in me, it is in Christ, and if I stay in Christ I have eternal life. He didn't give eternal life to me. It is still in him, as John says somewhere else. *This life is in his Son.* I don't have eternal life in me, but I do have it in Christ. A branch doesn't have life in itself. The vine has the life, and if the branch stays in the vine it will go on living, but if the branch gets cut off it will die. So I have eternal life in Christ. I don't have it in David Pawson. If I remain in Christ, I go on having eternal life.

That is what John 3:16 actually says. "For God so loved the world that he gave his only begotten Son that whoever goes on believing in him will never perish, but go on having eternal life." [My translation – the original Greek has those verbs in present continuous tense.] There it is. If you remain in Christ you have life, but if you don't, you'll die. The dead branches are gathered and thrown into the fire. Now that is just one passage and that is in the same Gospel where you read Jesus saying, "I know my sheep and none will pluck them out of my hand." You need to balance it up with this passage and take the whole truth together. The whole Gospel tells you the whole truth.

Let me now turn to Romans. I have already quoted that wonderful verse: "In all these things we are more than conquerors through him who loved us. For I'm convinced that neither death nor life, neither angels nor demons, neither the present nor the future, nor any powers, neither height nor depth, nor anything else in all creation will be able to separate us from the love of God which is in Christ Jesus our Lord." Wonderful promise, but now turn just one page, and let us read chapter 11 in which Paul is talking to Gentile believers about the Jews. He points out that not all the Jews made it. In fact, out of two and a half million Jews who left Egypt, two made it into the Promised Land. Paul, in a letter to Corinthians, says that is a lesson for us to learn. Setting out from Egypt is only the beginning. Getting into Canaan was the end of his redemption for them, but most of them never made it. He said that is a warning to us. It is not setting out, it is getting in. It is not starting, it is finishing that is going to be the thing.

So having talked about some of the Jews, many of whom were cut out of God's people one way or another, he says in v. 18, "Do not boast over those branches. [The Jews who were cut out.] If you do, consider this: you do not support the root, but the root supports you. You will say then, 'Branches were broken off so that I could be grafted in.' Granted. But they were broken off because of unbelief, and you stand by faith. Don't be arrogant, but be afraid. For if God did not spare the natural branches, he will not spare you either. Consider therefore the kindness and sternness of God: sternness to those who fell, but kindness to you, provided that you continue in his kindness. Otherwise, you also will be cut off."

He is talking about the Jews to the Gentile believers in Jesus. He said they were cut off, but don't let that make you arrogant or secure, because God will deal with you in the same way he dealt with them. He is the same God and if you do not continue in his kindness, you too will be cut off. I don't think you can twist those words around. They can only have one message, and it is that we are no more secure than the Jews were if we don't continue trusting in God.

That is a serious passage. How often have you heard it quoted by preachers? The big problem with all of us preachers is that we select the verses we preach on, and we don't preach on all of them. We select those, and if not careful we select those that we know that people like to hear – the comforting texts. We just keep the others a little bit quiet. I believe that we should be preaching the whole Bible, the whole Word of God, the whole counsel of God. In fact, Paul said to the Ephesians when he left Ephesus: "You know how I've taught you. I've declared to you the whole counsel of God, the whole truth."

In Hebrews 6 it actually says that if you turn away from Christ after you have belonged to him there is no possible repentance, no way back. I have been asked by some Christians: "How far do you have to backslide before you can't come back?" I say, "That's a dangerous question; don't even run the risk." There was a rich lady in England who advertised for a chauffeur to drive her Rolls Royce. She asked each applicant for the post, "How near could you drive to the cliff edge without the car going over?" One applicant said, "Well, I would go about six feet from the edge." Another said, "I would go about three feet." But one applicant said, "Madam, you are so valuable that I wouldn't go near a cliff edge," and he got the job. To ask how far I have to backslide before I reach the point of no return is someone playing with fire. That is someone saying, "How near can I get without going over?" It is the wrong question. Don't go anywhere near that. Don't backslide because it's quite clear from Bible teaching that there *is* a point of no return. I don't know what that point is. Only God knows, but don't run the risk. Don't even think about how far you have to backslide. Stay right there in Christ.

Chapter 6 I have noted already, finishes: even though we speak like this, dear friends, we are confident of better things in your case. Though he is giving them a warning of the point of no return, he says, "I'm confident..." not certain: I'm confident that you won't go anywhere near that point. But God's patience can run out, and we need to remember that.

Let us turn to chapter 10, where there is to me a far more serious warning, though many people have not noticed it. Verse 26: "If we deliberately keep on sinning after we have received the knowledge of the truth, no sacrifice for sins is left, but only a fearful expectation of judgment and of raging fire that will consume the enemies of God. Anyone who rejected the law of Moses died without mercy on the testimony of two or three witnesses. How much more severely do you think a man deserves to be punished who has trampled the Son of God under foot, who has treated as an unholy thing the blood of the covenant that sanctified him, and who has insulted the Spirit of grace? For we know him who said, 'It is mine to avenge; I will repay,' and again, 'The Lord will judge his people.' It is a dreadful thing to fall into the hands of the living God." A verse or two further he says: "So don't throw away your confidence."

Now that is a serious word. Pay careful attention. If you deliberately keep on sinning after you have received the knowledge of the truth, not even the cross of Christ is available for that. He is echoing the book of Leviticus. All the sacrifices in Leviticus were for accidental sin, unintended sin that you just fell into but didn't intend to. Then you brought a sacrifice for unintended sin, but here we are dealing with someone who quite deliberately, knowing what they are doing, having the knowledge of the truth, goes on living in the same way, and therefore cutting himself off from the efficacy of the cross. That is a serious warning.

Consider one other passage: 2 Peter 2:20. "If they have escaped the corruption of the world by knowing our Lord and Saviour Jesus Christ and are again entangled in it and overcome, they are worse off at the end than they were at the beginning. It would have been better for them not to have known the way of righteousness than to have known it and then to turn their backs on the sacred command that was passed on to them. Of them the proverbs are true: 'A dog returns to its vomit,' and 'a sow that is washed goes back to wallowing in mud.'" I wonder if you have ever heard a sermon on that passage. To say to someone: if, having escaped from the world by knowing Jesus is your Saviour, you then go back to the old way of life, you are worse off than if you had never known the way of salvation. Now if backsliding simply robbed you of your reward in heaven but you were still able to go there, then frankly you are not worse off than you were before. This is saying you are worse off. To have started the Christian life and escaped from the world and then go back into it, you are worse off because you are more responsible now. You have known the way of salvation, and now you have turned your back on it and you knew what it did for you.

That is a very serious warning and one that we should

note in scripture, God's Word. Therefore, people who have started and known the liberty in Christ, the freedom from sin that he offered, and then go back – it is characteristic of dogs when they vomit that they go back and lick up the sick, and I know what pig farmers are like. I know what pigs are like. Given the right care of pigs they are one of the cleanest animals on the farm, but not given the right care they just love to go back. When you have washed them clean, perhaps for an agricultural show, and they look beautiful and pink and nice, put them anywhere near some mud and they go right back into it. Peter here says you are worse off than if you had never known, which does not mean you are still going to heaven but will lose a bit of reward, it means you are not going to heaven. You have known the freedom that Christ can bring and now you have turned your back on it.

I could take you to eighty passages in the New Testament like these! One passage from every writer of the New Testament has a warning in it like that somewhere. If you read the Gospels, Jesus gave that warning more than once. When he told the parable of the sower, he said it is possible to receive the word of the kingdom and for it to begin to grow in you and then for it to be choked by the cares of this world. Warning after warning in scripture, which we ignore at our peril.

David, are you trying to make us scared? Yes, because the fear of the Lord is the beginning of wisdom. The New Testament doesn't leave the fear of the Lord behind in the Old. It is there in the New as well, again and again: fear of the Lord. What is there to fear from the Lord? The answer is "hell". When I wrote that book on hell, I said in it: "I fear hell." I'm not one of those preachers who say, "You unbelievers are all going to hell, but I'm going to heaven; blow you, Jack. I'm all right." I cannot preach like that. I can only preach on hell because I fear going there myself. I fear, as Paul said, "Lest having preached to others I should be cast away myself." It is a very healthy fear.

When we brought up three children we wanted to teach them fear of a healthy kind, not phobia. A phobia is when fear paralyses you and so dominates you that you can't move, can't do anything. We wanted our three children to be afraid of the traffic on the roads. We wanted them to have a healthy fear. We didn't give them bicycles until they had that healthy fear of traffic. One of our daughters was involved in a very bad accident. She escaped, but others didn't. We taught them to have a healthy fear, a fear of dirt, a fear of infection, but a healthy fear. It becomes a phobia if your children don't ride their bicycles on the road, but a healthy fear and they can go. You taught your children healthy fear, and the Bible does. There is a healthy fear of the Lord. It is related to the fear of his judgment, the fear of final rejection. That is a healthy fear and we need more of it.

The one thing I miss in so many churches I go to is the fear of the Lord. There is a kind of "pally-ness" with God that is very disturbing. One young man said to me, "We worship God all-matey in our church." I am afraid that summarises quite a lot of worship, as if we are partying with God and he is a great guy and we're having great fun with him. "It is a fearful thing," said the author of Hebrews, "to fall into the hands of the living God." I have heard preacher after preacher twist that verse and say, "It's a fearful thing to fall out of the hands of the living God." That may be true, but in that verse it says, "It's a fearful thing to fall into the hands of the living God." Occasionally I have preached in churches where people have trembled in the presence of God.

One group of Christians who did tremble before God were called the Quakers, because they literally shook in their meetings as they realised that God Almighty was there. They are now called the Society of Friends. The word "Quakers" went out of use, but it was the early Quakers from where I lived in Buckinghamshire, England who went out and established Pennsylvania. It was a man called Penn from a village next to where we lived in England who went out and took Quakerism to one of the northeastern US states: William Penn; Pennsylvania. He was a Quaker. He belonged to a people who were so aware of the presence of God. Paul says, "Work out your salvation with fear and trembling because God is working in you." When did you last see someone working out their salvation in fear and trembling because they realised Almighty God was doing something in them?

Well, I am just throwing this out. I know I am emphasising one side of things, but it is the side that has been neglected, because it is the side that people don't want to hear about. I promised the Lord when I began to preach, "Lord, I want to give people what they need to hear, not what they want to hear" – because I care for the people I speak to. I want to give you what you need to hear, and these are things you need to hear. Now of course, this raises a lot of questions in people's minds. One of those questions is the question of assurance, so let me deal with that. "Do you mean, David, that we can't be sure of salvation, that we can't be sure of God's love? Do you mean we have to wake up every morning wondering whether we're still in or out?" No, that's neurotic. I don't wake up every morning asking: "Am I saved or am I not, or am I going to be saved or am I not?" God wants us to be sure of him – sure of his purpose in you.

The New Testament is full of assuring promises to give you an assurance, but many Christians that I talk to are basing their assurance on the wrong thing. They want a written guarantee in the Word of God that will give them assurance. You see, *many people don't want to be saved, but they do want to be safe*. Do you know what I mean by that? They are coming into faith as if they are taking out a life insurance policy. They have been asked: "If you die tonight, will you be in heaven or hell?" and they don't want to be in hell so they take out a life insurance policy. They are assured from the Bible that they are safe. You are not safe until you get there, but you can be sure that you're going, because our assurance is not based on the promises of scripture. The early Christians didn't have the scripture, they didn't have the New Testament, so they didn't base their assurance on the scripture. The assurance is based on the Spirit – not the scripture but on the Spirit. It is the Spirit himself who bears witness that we are the sons of God, and while we walk in the Spirit we shall be sure where we are going. As soon as you are not walking in the Spirit and start walking your own way, you will lose your assurance. That is how you know when you are getting out of God's way. As long as you are on the way of salvation and the Spirit is leading you, you will have a witness in your Spirit that you are on the way to heaven and that as you keep on the way it is bound to get you there. I am putting that in a very simple manner. It is as if the satnav is telling you: "You're on the right road. Just keep on this road and you're certain to arrive." That is the kind of assurance the Bible offers you. It is an assurance from the Holy Spirit. He is the source of my assurance, and if I grieve the Spirit the first thing that goes is my sureness, my assurance that I am on the right way.

That is my understanding of assurance, and the witness of the Spirit will be borne out by the witness of my conscience. If you read John's first letter you will find it is full of this phrase "that you may know" and he points to the Spirit first. How do we know? Because he has given us his Spirit. There it is. How do we know? Because our conscience is witnessing that we are living a new life. The two witnesses – of the Spirit within us and the conscience in us – are going to make us very, very sure we are on the way to heaven. That is my understanding of assurance, not the kind of deduction from a text that says: the Bible says so; I believe it; that settles it. That is not a guarantee. It is not the assurance that we are offered. There is no absolute guarantee that you will make it, but you can still be very sure that you are on the way of salvation that leads to heaven.

So that is one question I get asked when I talk about being saved and being sure that you are being saved. Notice I don't say, "We are sure that we have been saved," but, "We are sure we are being saved." We know within our hearts from conscience and the Spirit within us. I am on the way, and I will get there if I keep on this way. It is that little word *if*. Underline that in your Bible—every text that puts an "if" in it. For example, in the beginning of 1 Corinthians 15 we find Paul outlining the essentials of the Christian faith. There are three. He says the death of Christ, the burial of Christ and the resurrection of Christ. These are the three fundamentals of the faith. He says, "This is the gospel I preached to you, which you received and on which you have taken your stand. By this gospel you are being saved, *if* you hold firmly to the word I preached to you."

That is one of the "if" verses, and I could quote so many more that have that little word "if" in them. There is an "if" and it is always followed by an exhortation to hang on, to hold firmly, to press on. You are in a race, and it is no good saying, "I've started the race, so I'm guaranteed to finish it." No, you press on to the end of the race, and you reach the end of the race. That is what Jesus did. Even when the worst happened to Jesus, he pressed on. In spite of the shame that he was subject to, he pressed on, he came through, and he finished. He was able to say on the cross: "It's finished."

I was given a prophecy many years ago when I was very uncertain about the future. It was about 1980. I was the minister of a "successful" church in England and things were going very well. I knew that the church needed to move forward into the 1980s, but I couldn't see my own place in it. I went away on a retreat with about a hundred pastors and I said, "Lord, will you please tell me this week whether I'm to go on leading this church or whether you have something else for me to do." There I was. Normally a pastor in that situation, having built new premises and filled them and got everything going, would want to stay there the rest of his life, but I wanted to do what the Lord wanted.

One of the speakers in that retreat, when he finished talking to us, said, "I have a word from the Lord for four men here. I don't know who they are, but you will know whether you're one of the men that God wants to speak to." He proceeded to give three words from the Lord, not one of which made any sense to me. Then he said, "My son, you have ministered to the extent of your gift in the place where I certainly put you. You are no longer bound to stay in that place. I set the land before you, but one thing I require of you: that you surrender all that remains to be done in that church into my hands, for it is my church, not yours." That prophecy – every word was going through my heart. He finished by saying, "I want you to go out and so serve me so that one day you will be able to look into my face and say, 'Lord, we did it.'"

Lovely word! I took a recording of it home to the elders of the church. I said, "I'm submitting that to you. I believe it was for me, but you've got to weigh and judge it. I'm not going to respond to that unless you confirm it." The elders came back to me and said, "We believe that's of the Lord. We'll let you go." I went out into the unknown, and yet within two years I had spoken in two hundred cities and towns in Britain, and I have been travelling ever since. I am a tramp for the Lord, but that has been going on. Here I am. I believe I am in God's will, and I tell you this: it is not boring, serving the Lord, but it is tiring. But I believe I am doing what God wanted me to do.

The other question I have often been asked is: how can you be sure? How can you have assurance under what you are teaching? I have said I believe you can, but it is not the kind of written guarantee people want. It is an inward assurance from the Holy Spirit and your conscience that you are on the right track that leads to heaven. If you stay on that track you will make it, you will get there.

Another question I get asked about is the question of *predestination*. Now it is a word in scripture. I believe in the predestination of God, but people say, "If God has predestined something for you, surely it is bound to happen." No, I believe that is a misunderstanding of the word "predestination", treating it as if it is the same as predetermination. That is a very different word. Unfortunately, most people don't see the difference. To predetermine something is to make it happen, to force it to happen. It is bound to happen if it is predetermined, but God does not predetermine, he predestines.

What is predestination? It is preparing a destiny for someone. I can give you a very simple illustration. I grew up with an ambition to be a farmer. When I left school at sixteen, I went on to a farm and worked on it. You may not believe it, but I used to get up at four in the morning to milk ninety cows. I couldn't do it now, but that is where I got my complexion, working in the open air!

Well, I enjoyed working on the farm, and I thought, "Where will this career lead?" One day my father called me into his study, for he was a professor of agriculture in the university. He said, "David, I know you've wanted to be a farmer, and I'm sharing this with you now, that when you're twenty-one, I've arranged for you to rent a farm for yourself." I was terribly grateful to him for thinking of that, but I said, "I'm sorry; I can't do that, because a few weeks ago my heavenly Father told me to be a preacher." It had happened in this way. I was already preaching, but not in churches, in the open air, down at the beach, outside cinema queues, wherever people gathered. My pulpit was an old American army jeep. I would park it, stand up in the back and preach. I just wanted the world to know about Jesus.

So it came to the point one morning when I said, "Lord, if you tell me by twelve o'clock today which you want me to be, preacher or farmer, I'll be what you want me to be." All my forebears had been preachers or farmers or both, right back to John Wesley. I said, "Tell me by mid-day today, and I'll do what you want." That's the kind of guidance I have found to be so useful, and I don't do anything unless God clearly tells me. It is his responsibility to guide me. It's not my responsibility to try to read his mind. That is my thinking about guidance. I told the Lord, "If you will tell me clearly what you want me to do, I'll do it. If you tell me clearly where to go, I'll go there. If you tell me clearly what to say, I'll say it, but you're my boss and you've got to tell me. Then you know I'll do it." I've kept my side of the bargain, and he has kept his. It is his responsibility.

Which of you going into work on a Monday morning, would have a boss coming to you and saying, "Guess what I want you to do today?" No, if the boss wants you to do something on Monday morning, he will come and tell you. If he doesn't come and tell you, you assume that he wants you to do on Monday what you did on Friday and to carry on where you are. Don't move unless the Lord tells you clearly. Carry on doing what you are doing until he clearly says, "Change of job; change of location" – whatever. I have found that is important. Too many Christians put themselves in the place where they have got to have guidance and got to do something and got to find it somehow, twisting God's arm until he tells them what he wants them to do. Don't change anything until he tells you to. Then change, and it works beautifully. If you get impatient and drop your job or leave the place where you are and then try to find something else that the Lord wants you to do, you are in trouble. Don't move until the Lord says "Move."

So that morning I said, "Lord, if you want me to be a preacher or a farmer or even both, tell me by mid-day today." At ten-thirty I was having coffee with a friend, who was also working on the farm, and he looked at me and he said, "David, you won't finish up behind a plough. You'll finish up in a pulpit."

I said, "Lord, that's not clear enough." I left my friend, went out into the street, in the city of Newcastle in the northeast of England, and I could take you almost to the very stone on which I was standing when I met a retired Methodist minister whom I hadn't seen for years and years. I said to him, "Mr. Scott, lovely to see you again. How are you?" He didn't answer. He just said, "David, why aren't you in the ministry?" I said, "That's clear enough, Lord."

So I never got the farm that my father had prepared for me, but if I had taken that farm I could always have said, "My father predestined me to be a farmer here." Do you understand what I am saying? He did not predetermine it. In fact I said no, but had I said yes I could have talked about predestination: what my father decided beforehand should be my destiny. That is what predestination means. It doesn't mean that God treats me like a puppet and predetermines me to do that. When I accept his plan – and it is a much better plan than mine – I can say, "He predestined." He prepared the plan. I've accepted it, and I now know that long before I accepted it, he had planned it all.

As I look back over my life, I am not proud of many things. I have regrets, but his plan for me has been absolutely right.

He predestined me for that. He had the plan long before I knew it, but at the age of seventeen I submitted to that plan and said, "Okay, Lord, I'll do what you want." I have no regrets about that. In fact, I wouldn't change places with anybody. It is lovely to reach the end of your life and realise that you did keep to the plan God had for you. He tailors the plan to each person, and I can see that even before I accepted his plan he was preparing me for it. As a young farmer we had what we called Young Farmers' Club. They had speaking competitions, and I began to learn to speak in public before I became a Christian. God was using the Young Farmers' Club debates to prepare me to speak clearly and convincingly. I can see he had the plan. He was preparing me for the plan and the plan for me.

That is predestination, and I love it, but it is not predetermination. He didn't force me to do it. I could have resisted it. I could have said no to my heavenly Father and yes to my earthly father, and I would be a farmer milking cows right now. I have no regrets because farming has become a real problem activity in our country. Many farmers are committing suicide because they are finding it difficult to make a living. I don't regret it for that reason. I regret not being a farmer because I loved it, I enjoyed it, but I still wouldn't go back and make any other decision. So predestination fits in as well.

I must be drawing this to a close. The fear of the Lord is part of our walk with God. One day, when we are perfect in love, all fear will go. There will be no need for it. Perfect love casts out fear, but as long as your love is imperfect there is a healthy fear of not making it. That does not make me neurotic. I don't get up every morning wondering if I am a Christian, but I know if I get out of that way of God and my assurance begins to go, thank you Lord for warning me – I will get back on the road quickly.

That is why John Bunyan wrote a book called *The Pilgrim's Progress*. I hope you will read it. He saw the Christian life as a Way, a road. People began on that road and slipped off it, and when Pilgrim gets to the River Jordan at the end of the road and he sees the Heavenly City in the distance, and he realises all he needs do is cross that river, he has a friend with him. That friend looks at the river rather than the city, and he says, "That river's deep and it's dark and it's dangerous. I don't like to try crossing it." The friend turns to the left, and there is a path leading away. The friend leaves Pilgrim and goes down the path. John Bunyan writes this: "I saw then that there is a road to hell even from the gates of heaven." That is where I got the title of my book *The Road to Hell*. Even at the end of your pilgrimage you could still get off the road. Perhaps when you get to my age, you have to be doubly careful not to let things go and get off that road but to finish triumphantly.

My favourite hymn writer is Charles Wesley. His hymns are full of scripture. In an eight line verse you can have sixteen verses of scripture mentioned. He was soaked in the Bible, and he had a great gift of poetry. Somebody once told me, "If you can't find a hymn of Charles Wesley for them to sing after you have preached, you have to ask, 'Should I have preached on that?'" He covered the whole Bible in six thousand wonderful songs. We have lost most of them, but there is one quite short song he wrote. I want to quote it to prove that I have been teaching the right stuff because he wrote a hymn for it.

Ah Lord, with trembling I confess,
A gracious soul may fall from grace;
The salt may lose its seasoning power,
And never, never, find it more.
Lest that my fearful case should be,
Each moment knit my soul to thee;
And lead me to the mount above,
Through the low vale of humble love.

That is my message. I am afraid the vast majority of evangelical preachers would not preach what I have taught here. Don't believe it because I have said it. Don't say, "Do you know what David Pawson says?" Don't you dare use my name! Study the Word of God. Get into your Bible and find out whether what I have told you is there. Then go and tell people what the Bible says, what the Word of God says.

ABOUT
DAVID
PAWSON

A speaker and author with uncompromising faithfulness to the Holy Scriptures, David brings clarity and a message of urgency to Christians to uncover hidden treasures in God's Word.

Born in England in 1930, David began his career with a degree in Agriculture from Durham University. When God intervened and called him to become a Minister, he completed an MA in Theology at Cambridge University and served as a Chaplain in the Royal Air Force for three years. He moved on to pastor several churches, including the Millmead Centre in Guildford, which became a model for many UK church leaders. In 1979, the Lord led him into an international ministry. His current itinerant ministry is predominantly to church leaders. David and his wife Enid currently reside in the county of Hampshire in the UK.

Over the years, he has written a large number of books, booklets, and daily reading notes. His extensive and very accessible overviews of the books of the Bible have been published and recorded in *Unlocking the Bible*. Millions of copies of his teachings have been distributed in more than 120 countries, providing a solid biblical foundation.

He is reputed to be the "most influential Western preacher in China" through the broadcast of his best-selling *Unlocking the Bible* series into every Chinese province by Good TV. In the UK, David's teachings are often broadcast on Revelation TV.

Countless believers worldwide have also benefited from his generous decision in 2011 to make available his extensive audio video teaching library free of charge at www.davidpawson.org and we have recently uploaded all of David's video to a dedicated channel on www.youtube.com

TAKE A LOOK AT YOUTUBE
www.youtube.com/user/DavidPawsonMinistry

THE EXPLAINING SERIES
BIBLICAL TRUTHS SIMPLY EXPLAINED

If you have been blessed reading this book, there are more available in the series. Please register to download more booklets for free by visiting **www.explainingbiblicaltruth.global**

Other booklets in the *Explaining* series will include:
The Amazing Story of Jesus
The Resurrection: *The Heart of Christianity*
Studying the Bible
Being Anointed and Filled with the Holy Spirit
New Testament Baptism
How to study a book of the Bible: Jude
The Key Steps to Becoming a Christian
What the Bible says about Money
What the Bible says about Work
Grace – *Undeserved Favour, Irresistible Force
or Unconditional Forgiveness?*
Eternally secure? – *What the Bible says about being saved*
De-Greecing the Church – The impact of Greek thinking
on Christian beliefs
Three texts often taken out of context:
Expounding the truth and exposing error
The Trinity
The Truth about Christmas

They will also be avaiable to purchase as print copies from:
Amazon or **www.thebookdepository.com**

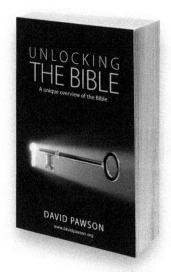

UNLOCKING
THE BIBLE

A unique overview of both the Old and New Testaments, from internationally acclaimed evangelical speaker and author David Pawson. *Unlocking the Bible* opens up the Word of God in a fresh and powerful way. Avoiding the small detail of verse by verse studies, it sets out the epic story of God and his people in Israel. The culture, historical background and people are introduced and the teaching applied to the modern world. Eight volumes have been brought into one compact and easy to use guide to cover both the Old and New Testaments in one massive omnibus edition. *The Old Testament: The Maker's Instructions* (The five books of law); *A Land and A Kingdom* (Joshua, Judges, Ruth, 1&2 Samuel, 1&2 Kings); *Poems of Worship and Wisdom* (Psalms, Song of Solomon, Proverbs, Ecclesiastes, Job); *Decline and Fall of an Empire* (Isaiah, Jeremiah and other prophets); *The Struggle to Survive* (Chronicles and prophets of exile); *The New Testament: The Hinge of History* (Mathew, Mark, Luke, John and Acts); *The Thirteenth Apostle* (Paul and his letters); *Through Suffering to Glory* (Hebrews, the letters of James, Peter and Jude, the Book of Revelation). Already an international bestseller.

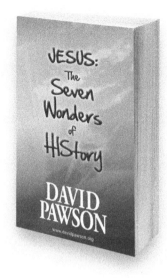

JESUS:
THE SEVEN
WONDERS
OF HISTORY

This book is the result of a lifetime of telling 'the greatest story ever told' around the world. David re-told it to many hundreds of young people in Kansas City, USA, who heard it with uninhibited enthusiasm, 'tweeting' on the internet about 'this cute old English gentleman' even while he was speaking.

Taking the middle section of the Apostles' Creed as a framework, David explains the fundamental facts about Jesus on which the Christian faith is based in a fresh and stimulating way. Both old and new Christians will benefit from this 'back to basics' call and find themselves falling in love with their Lord all over again.

OTHER TEACHINGS
BY DAVID PAWSON

For the most up to date list of David's Books
go to: **www.davidpawsonbooks.com**

To purchase David's Teachings
go to: **www.davidpawson.com**

Lightning Source UK Ltd.
Milton Keynes UK
UKHW020739280722
406510UK00010B/878